The Shadow and the Light

The Shadow and the Light

Selected Poems, 1946-1999

S. P. Dunn

Highgate Road Social Science Research Station
Berkeley, California
2000

Copyright © Ethel Dunn, 2000
ISBN 0-9707190-0-0

Front cover: S.P. Dunn, 1950
Back cover: S.P. Dunn, 1980

Edited by Ethel Dunn
Design by Albert R. Vogeler
Printed by Brea Printing, Brea, California

Highgate Road Social Science Research Station
32 Highgate Road
Berkeley, CA 94707

ACKNOWLEDGMENTS

"Sonnet in Free Rhythm," "Contemporary Sonnet," "Norway Harbor," "Tarquinia: Carmen Etrusca," and "Upon the Calendar: for New Year's 1954" were published in *Some Watercolors from Venice and Other Poems*, Riverdale, New York: The Coalbin Press, 1956.

"From Hospital" was published in *The Antioch Review*, September 1957, Volume 17, No. 3, pp. 374-378, except for the substitution of a different sixth poem.

"The Umbrella-Pine, Nervi, August '53" and "Gothic Saint, Battisteria, Pisa" were published in *Erehwon*, April 1980, #101, pp. 10 and 14 respectively.

"Deo Gratia: The Recluse," "On the Gray Hill" and "The Cat of Bastet" were published in *Erehwon*, October 1980, No. 102, pp. 11, 19, and 24 respectively.

"With Me through Summer Woods" and "Appearances of Things: From the Patio, Sunny Afternoon in Late March" were published in *Erehwon*, April 1981, No. 103, pp. 37 and 42 respectively.

"Cypress" was published as part of "Two Tree Invocations" in *Eras Review*, Spring 1981, p. 53.

"The Hummingbird: A Lesson in Optics," was published in *Connecticut River Review*, Spring 1981, Volume 3, No. 1, p. 13.

"The Greenland Fishermen" was published in *Guts & Grace*, Summer 1981, pp. 40-41.

"Summer Evening in the Suburbs, Waiting for a Movie" was published in *The Pikestaff Forum*, Spring 1983, No. 5, p. 5.

"Dream Vision" was published in *Métier*, Fall 1984, p. 8.

"Chinese Painting: Travellers in a Mountain Pass," was published in *Blue Unicorn*, February 1987, Volume X, No. 2, p. 18.

"The Road to the Mountain" was published in slightly different form in *Kaleidoscope: International Magazine of Literature, Fine Arts, and Disability*, Winter/Spring, 1989, No. 18, pp. 38-39.

"Immigration File" was published, in slightly altered form, in *Kaleidoscope: International Magazine of Literature, Fine Arts, and Disability*, 1996, No. 32, pp. 29-30.

DEDICATION

To my beloved teachers
Mark Van Doren
B. J. R. Stolper
Gerd (Ralph G.) Victor

CONTENTS

FOREWORD 1
PREFACE 2
INTRODUCTION 5
To Anne 11
Contemporary Sonnet 12
Sonnet in Free Rhythm 13
Sonnet: With Me through Summer Woods 14
Sea-Sonnet 15
Norway Harbor 16
The Labor of Poetry 17
Upon the Calendar: for New Year's 1954 18
Song of High Summer 19
Trivial Elegy 20
Invocation: Carmina Burana 21
Hart's Island Elegy: A Fragment 22
Voluntary for a Memorial Service 24
Classic Earth: Record of an Italian Journey
    1. The Umbrella-Pine, Nervi, August '53 25
    2. Gothic Saint, Battisteria, Pisa 25
    3. Cypress 26
    4. On the Gray Hill 26
    5. Statue of Saint Cecilia in Her Tomb, Rome 26
    6. Roman Etching: Piazza Navona 27

7. Tarquinia: Carmen Etrusca 28
8. The Bound Slaves of Buonarotti, Vatican Museum 29

The Dying Meditation of Giovanni Pico Della Mirandola, Called
    the Phoenix of Intellects 32

Poem for a Modern Wedding 36

The Con-Game: Classical Ode on the Unreality of All Things ..38

From Hospital

    1. Night on the Ward 39
    2. Death and Bingo 39
    3. Delirium 40
    4. The Orderly 40
    5. This Seeing the Sick: For Ruben 41
    6. In the Next Bed 41
    7. Visiting-Hours 42
    8. Escape 43

Procession at Peredelkino: The Funeral of Boris Pasternak, from a
    Photograph 44

The Road to the Mountain 45

The Cat of Bastet 49

Deo Gratia: The Recluse 50

Chinese Painting: Travellers in a Mountain Pass 51

Back Yard, Berkeley, Late March 52

Chicago Hash-House Nocturne, Mid-November 53

The Greenland Fishermen 54

The Hummingbird: A Lesson in Optics 55

Dream Vision: A Door Opens 56
Appearances of Things: From the Patio, Sunny Afternoon in Late
    March 57
The Problem of the Nth Jumper 58
The City of Early Fall: Old Man in the Park 59
Summer Evening in the Suburbs, Waiting for a Movie 60
Nocturnes 61
Litany of the Two Worlds 63
The Shadow and the Light 65
Seeing Angels 66
The Failed Prophet 67
Immigration File 68
Preludes
    1. Dreams of the Maimed 71
    2. Moment of Silence, Please 71
The Well-Behaved Old Man's Half-Lament for His Old Age 73
Fourfold Prayer 74
Voices from a War Zone 75
ABOUT THE AUTHOR 77

FOREWORD

S. P. Dunn (Stephen Porter Dunn)—my husband, died unexpectedly on June 4, 1999, before these poems could be published. I had meant to print them as far back as 1996, but then there seemed to be all the time in the world. "The Dying Meditation of Giovanni Pico Della Mirandola, Called the Phoenix of Intellects" was written when Stephen was in college, and it was read at his memorial by his best friend, Al Vogeler, to whom the poem had been dedicated. The dying scholar's meditation, minus the Roman Catholicism, is very much the mind-set of Stephen himself. Many of his last poems seemed to envision his own death. "Fourfold Prayer" reminds me of Stephen's last minutes. Several weeks before his death, Stephen wrote "Voices from a War Zone," and in keeping with his chronological scheme, I have made it the last poem in this collection. He did not have the energy to proofread the poem, but it says so much about his sense of justice that I include it as if he meant others to see it. Stephen often said that the person who wrote the poems, S. P. Dunn, was not the same person who had a rich and distinguished scholarly career as a cultural anthropologist, editor, and translator of Russian social sciences, but to me they are one and the same, informed by the same grace, elegance and passion. This book honors the memory of a man gone too soon.

My thanks to Janice Dunn, Stephen's sister-in-law, for producing the original computer text of the poems; to Al Vogeler for editing, design, and work with the printer; to Elizabeth Cirocco and David Jones of Advance Graphix; and to Maria Sakovich for her keen eye in proofreading.

Ethel Dunn

PREFACE

In view of the considerable time-span which these poems cover, it wouldn't be surprising if some readers got the impression that they were written by two entirely different poets, rather than by one at different stages of his life, as is in fact the case. For this reason, I have arranged the poems in roughly chronological order, to show the change as it took place. Yet, there is a sense in which the reader's factually erroneous first impression would be correct: there was a period of almost twenty-five years during which I wrote almost no completed poems. It goes without saying that the person who emerged from this period of silence and self-imposed (or semi-voluntary) exile was quite different from the one who had gone into it—older and certainly sadder, if not necessarily wiser. It seems to me that the new poems show a receding of the lyrical impulse (except in a few cases) and a strengthening of the reflective—or ironic, or philosophical—one, which is sometimes considered characteristic of advancing age.

S. P. Dunn

INTRODUCTION

Stephen Porter Dunn, 1928-1999

Remarks at a Memorial Service at Friends Meeting House,
Berkeley, California, July 31, 1999

Albert R. Vogeler

What I am about to say may come as something of a surprise to those of you who knew Stephen as a scholar here in Berkeley for the last ten, or twenty, or thirty years. I knew him for fifty years, and knew him best as a poet, a visionary, and a lover of literature, who happened only later to become an expert on Russian social thought and Marxist theory, an anthropologist, editor, and translator. His early zest for literature, in three, four or five languages, was so intense in our undergraduate and early graduate school years at Columbia that it awed and thrilled me.

He revealed to me, and a few others, how it was to be in thrall to the Muse. He took inspiration from poetry I had never heard of, and pronounced it slowly with the solemn rhythms of incantation. The verse he so completely assimilated came to him, line after line, upon the slightest prompting, as if from the poet's own lips. Keats, Browning, Hopkins, Eliot, Yeats, Auden, and Graves were among his models; Dante, Shakespeare, and Goethe were touchstones. It was Robert Graves' *The White Goddess* that reinforced and crystallized not only Stephen's feelings about poetic inspiration but also his interest in comparative mythology.

Stephen's friends found themselves thinking about literary works they would never have been tempted to read, only because Stephen attested to their importance. It was an additional education, in the midst of our college courses, to be inspired by *his* inspiration. Every poetry session with Stephen was for me an experience of new meaning and feeling, and a demonstration of his exquisitely-tuned mental and auditory apparatus. His three roommates next door in the Livingston Hall dorm from 1948 to 1952 thought he was a wonder—and left it at that. He was a phenomenon to me too, a genius gifted in spirit and mind in over-compensation for his cruel physical disability. It was often painful for me to talk with him when the play of his mind could not be rapidly vocalized—and terribly ironic, since articulate speech and song were so important to him (as were his other vicarious loves, the performance of music and dance). Yet our talk was not all serious or strained. We discussed politics and social policy (he had an acute sense of social justice), gossiped about academic personalities, and found humor in unexpected places illuminated by his associative memory and quirky insight. Gales of unconstrained laughter often swept our rooms. And then there were those cozy weekends when I visited him in his parents' book-lined home in Riverdale for long conversations around the fire with his father and often other scholars from the University.

Stephen's early poetry, like that of any young poet, reveals the shaping influences of his reading, and he was exceedingly conscious of traditions, of models, of form. He experimented all the time in various modes, and every so often would give us something new—a few lines, or a few pages. "The Labor of Poetry," "Sonnet in Free Rhythm," and "Contemporary Sonnet" were, I recall, read aloud to us soon after their completion. Stephen could reach heights of great eloquence and poignancy when he allowed himself to speak unabashedly in the voice of the poets he loved best. "Tarquinia: Carmen Etrusca," written after a trip to Italy, reminds us of the haunting cadences of Keats' "Ode on a Grecian Urn," and celebrates a similar survival of beauty in the face of death.

It is not really surprising that Stephen dwelt chiefly with love and death and fate and beauty, the great themes of poetry, things just beyond our comprehension. As a victim of fate, he responded with stoicism and irony; and his knowledge, courage, and imagination took him from his wheelchair soaring into the great realms of high culture. He was a stoic in the deepest sense, resigned to mortal reality but living, through his mind, beyond it. He was a stoic lyricist, a connoisseur of irony, an ironist of love. Doing and not doing, having and not having, were the opposite poles of his poetic consciousness, just as they surely mirrored the struggle within his physical being. But knowing and not knowing, believing and not believing, were even more important themes. He was a conscientious agnostic when agnosticism was an admission of ignorance and a badge of honesty; he was a conflicted agnostic when he wanted to believe something but found nothing to believe, or found his old beliefs untenable. He could pose, poetically, as a religious believer, to see what believing was like, and as a non-believer, to feel the void. He hovered often at the edge of some epiphany, perhaps glimpsing it, usually not. He was reverently, poignantly, expectant, and inured to disappointment. That was the epitome of his life as a poet as I saw it—or really, as I see it now, in retrospect.

But then, in the later 1950s, Stephen ceased to be an active poet. I never really came to terms with this, but respected his reticence. We graduated from Columbia College, he two years before me, and in due course we both went to graduate school at Columbia, married, and left New York. Though for his last thirty years we were only 400 miles apart in California, our dialogue was sporadic. Stephen's consuming interests, following his Columbia Ph.D. in anthropology under Margaret Mead, were the ethnography of the peoples of the Soviet Union, and Soviet Marxism. These and other Russian cultural studies he pursued with his wife Ethel in their heroically productive parallel careers of scholarship and translation. I was able to share their interests only to a degree, while Stephen continued to share mine in philosophy, religion, and history. But for many years we had only occasional serious discussions, like one about his book *The Fall and*

Rise of the Asiatic Mode of Production. Stephen was generously forgiving about my lapses in communication. During the last two decades of his life he began to write poetry again, less lyrical, more meditative, but with the same underlying irony and humane sympathies.

The Dunn family gradually passed away: his distinguished father, the geneticist L. C. Dunn; his brilliant brother Bob; his gracious mother Louise. Ethel remains Stephen's sole intellectual legatee. During all these years they remained intensely interactive collaborators at their unique intellectual outpost in the hills of Kensington, north of Berkeley, the Highgate Road Social Science Research Station. Ethel is also a notable scholar of Russian culture in her own right. My wife Martha and I have loved and admired her for forty years for her achievement, her devotion, and her fortitude. When I last spoke to Stephen, in May 1999, he characteristically asked what projects I had been pursuing, and would I send him a summary; and he promised to let me know about his and Ethel's current work. This interchange never occurred.

Stephen had always known how to relinquish a full life gracefully: he said it often in his poems. His Browningesque monologue written about 1950 and for years existing only in typescript, "The Dying Meditation of Giovanni Pico della Mirandola, Called the Phoenix of Intellects," captures the intellectual passion of the Renaissance Neoplatonic philosopher. Self-proclaimed master of all knowledge and bold seeker after ultimate truth, Pico dreamed of a synthesis of religious wisdom culminating in a final illumination. Pico's friends at his death, it is said, were convinced his gift was so precious that he must somehow live again, like the Phoenix, to inspire future generations with the greatness of the human spirit. Stephen understandably identified with Pico's consuming need to find meaning in his learning. He also shared Pico's doubts and distractions, and at the end, like Pico, humbly accepted his all-too-human frailty.

TO ANNE

O flame, O spear
Poised on the world's dark rim,
O rising brightness,
Upward arrow of light,
Grant me to live,
Like thee, in despite of darkness.

O resting, gentle flame,
Flickering upward,
O bright tree in the wind,
Grant me to be,
Like thee, a quiet weapon
In a strong hand, against darkness.

CONTEMPORARY SONNET

I honor the memory of all those who in these years
Died doing the right thing, but were mistaken,
And of those who deserted the right thing, torn and shaken
As it became the wrong thing. When the time clears
Like a misted glass in sunlight, and the guilt each bears
For his acid choice of evils—the word unspoken
That would have rendered justice, the covenant broken
For the best reasons—lifts itself and shares
Its burden more equally among us, then
Perhaps these many, bewildered now, can come
To their own peace and certainty again,
Know the true cause and the true battle. Some
Milleniums since, while a mad emperor raved,
Men even as these asked, What must we do to be saved?

SONNET IN FREE RHYTHM

Here, now, in the silence of language, in the gap
Between word and word, where the cool breeze blows through
Into the mind, I could say all to you
I've ever wanted to say, but I would rap
The message out like code; my tongue would tap
On the walls of my thought. This I could do,
As a bird, wordlessly. I would be two
Feet drumming the dumb ground, a hare in this trap.

And you would hear the melody along
A wind of silence, the bright ballad in the quiet sun,
The voice of light in the mind, for speech is song—
Even dumb speech on wood or earth—a song begun
In rhythm of air, a song of soft sounds flowing
Through spaces in loud words—a cool wind, like knowing.

SONNET: WITH ME THROUGH SUMMER WOODS

With me through summer woods where blackbirds make
Metallic ripples in the shimmering air,
A boy walks wordless—the boy I was—or there
Stands watching the swallows diving over the lake
For wingéd prey. In vain the sun cries: Wake!
Or the wind shifts, saying: That year's nowhere;
Leave it long drowned in memory, and fare
Forward light-hearted.
        Those saplings bend and shake
In wind not of this year, shine in sun long gone by
Over these blinding heavens with a crash;
The eagle's lone cold flight, the loon's far cry,
Mark *finis*,   as time burns to fragrant ash
And blows away.
        That endless summer's gone,
But that lost boy stands fixed there like a stone.

SEA-SONNET

What time does the wave keep?—or the small bird
Brainless and bold, and elegantly stepping
Between two depths, of sea and land, not slipping
Between two equal deaths? The clock unheard—
Sandfall in the sea's glass—without a word,
Tells but the one death: ours; and counts the leaping
Beasts of the water, which will kill us.   Hoping
Is a fool's game, and our small cries absurd
In sandy vastness.
        No; hope not to wake
Happier, freer, for on the shore of sleep
Flame cold as starfires licks out of the deep
And turns bones black with grief.
        Nothing can slake
Its burning, while the suffering flesh remains,
And mind inhabits it to know its pains.

NORWAY HARBOR

The skerries deny the great sea. Gull and goose
Wander perplexed in calm—winds slow, clouds loose,
Pastures gentle to water. And the bay,
Neat-shaped as cut with chisel, prisons day
Over its surface, pressed light within walls
Black with the absent sun. The spent sail falls,
Empty of travel. The raised oar lies along
The splintered gunwale.
       Breeze-breath in ear's a song,
Now rustle against the boat's side, cry from shore,
Now silence, poised and waiting, like the core
Of brown rock barring breakers, now no sound.
Clouds shaped like high harps humming, winds flow round.
Winds shape like running water. Pastures slide
Smoothly to darkness.
       Fall, oars; hurry; hide.

THE LABOR OF POETRY

Definition of things
And prayer to the things defined
Is the labor of poetry,
As if one said, as a child pointing:
"Tree. Water. Sky." And after:
"Tree, be fruitful. Water, flow.
Sky, be suspended above us, high and blue."
Observe: the prayer
Is not for a miracle or a breach of order,
But for the fact, the condition of existence,
That it persist and maintain us.
When we pray to the fact in its own behalf
It is unmoved, an integral shape of silence
Like an island
Beaten by a rushing surf of sound.

There is a still kernel at the root of the word—
A vacant chamber within which it echoes,
For the word is itself the echo of the fact
Mixed with the sound of the fact itself.
When the prophetic oaks rustle
Their silences carry the message.

UPON THE CALENDAR: FOR NEW YEAR'S 1954

We, with some few good friends,
Before, have celebrated,
Modestly, as befits this anniversary
Of our world, dedicated,
As we were
Always, to the idea of its
Continuance, and true to the groundless hope
From which we infer

Our further life, in spite
Of every wind and season,
Malice and folly of men, wars, insurrections,
Crimes, death without reason.
After one
More round of the solemn months, shall we
Find ourselves lodged once more in the same house,
Even as the sun,

Which to his accustomed seat
In the narrow skull returning,
Shines, somewhere in the cortex with a grayish light,
Like an old coin burning,
And keeps
All times, births, deaths, occasions, feasts
Imposed upon him by the law of Man
And never sleeps,
And finds himself at home
In the same place this year
As last, in the same heavens cold and dark with distance,
The same mind dark with fear?
What may,
For all our wish, not come to pass,
And for all our effort, not overwhelm us
Before the day?

SONG OF HIGH SUMMER

Wind, treetop-tall, the cicada's companion
Whispers among the leaves—
Black alder, poplar, silver-sided willow—
Tossing the sheaves
In heated air, in sunlight. Wind, treetop-tall
The turning earth begets,
But only while it turns; wind sinks to silence
When the sun sets.

Suspended in this world, the hawk hangs fire,
His feathers splayed for flight.
The moment kindles, climbs in flame. The hawk's eye,
Searching its light,
Discovers prey and leads him down. The fish,
Rising, shatters the lake's
Soft glass with thousand rings. Splash! and the sifting
Silence breaks.

TRIVIAL ELEGY

How faint, how brief
In the green wood
Are flower and leaf,
Sunlight not understood,
And small birds calling.
Of all things good
Last only sweet winds' grief
And slow rain falling.

INVOCATION: CARMINA BURANA

Out of the greenwood years, my masters, come,
    Harping and singing to a young-world tune,
        Dancing to flute and viol. *Cras amet*
        Qui nunquam amavit; he who loves not yet
    Shall love tomorrow, if there is one. Soon,
Birds to their nests, and Man to his long home,
And mourners in the streets; but for this while
Let loving be our song, and Fortune smile.

De ramis cadunt folia; desire shall fail,
As brown leaf from the bough, as wind from sail,
    As virtue and enchantment from this world,
        As you, my masters, vanished in the mists
        Of unremembrance out of which you came.
        And music only shall bring back the name
    You kept and carried, who, vanquished in the lists
Of Love and Fortune, held still your flags unfurled.

HART'S ISLAND ELEGY: A FRAGMENT

In memory of Louisa Van Slyke, "born at sea, died alone at Charity Hospital, aged 24," April 24, 1869 (the first person buried in the New York potter's field, on Hart's Island).

Then Judas, who had betrayed Him, when he saw that He was condemned, repented himself, and brought again the thirty pieces of silver to the chief priests. And they took counsel, and bought with them the potter's field, to bury strangers in. (Matt. 27: 3, 7).

Over the shining Sound the gull wheels high,
Bright-winged and terrible.
        Oh unhuman eye,
Staring at nothing out of a cold nowhere,
Recording only this moment, mind filled with lifting air,
Which only the sun inhabits, what do you know
Of us, quiet dead beneath? You come and go
As the one eye of blind heaven opens and closes,
Measuring us our light, or as the wind disposes
The salt-marsh grasses and the tangled willow
Above our low-roofed town. We stir on our pillow,
Remembering other winds in other seasons,
Which have ceased blowing, but we have forgotten the reasons
In our long absence.
        You have no memory
Nor sin nor sorrow—you, balanced on liberty,
A weightless white bird, the witness of resurrection.
We have forgotten the sun's course, and the tides' direction,
Beyond our windless harbor, and where we were going
When the storm thrust us here. Beneath the unknowing,
Uncaring sky, our different element
Stretches and heaves and settles, confused in movement,
Eternal and momentary, like the sea

On which it rests.
        We miss that liberty,
That sliding groundswell, almost not at all,
Because we seem to feel it still: rise, fall,
Rock, roll, rest, and again.
        Backward in the green light
Which filters through these waves—backward out of the night
Where strange fish pass and strange weeds float—we gaze,
From blank bone, across emptiness of days.

Hush; did we suffer once the troubling fire
Which those who suffer it call life? No higher
Than kelp or flotsam on the deserted beach,
Our beaten hopes now rise. Though we can reach
The once-forbidden fruit, forbidden no longer,
We have no wish for it. Caught in the stronger
Motion and music of the turning world,
What should we do with knowledge? The grub, close-curled
In the hard earth of winter, needs more than we,
Having his flights before him. Vacancy
Claims us, shot with vain winds and passing storms;
Such things as we ourselves are—scudding forms,
Shadows of shadows of insubstantial clouds—
Blow here and there in faceless, nameless crowds.

VOLUNTARY FOR A MEMORIAL SERVICE

(James Howard McGregor, 1869-1954; Department
of Zoology, Columbia University, 1894-1954).

Under the dome of Romanesque drab brick
Bare light bulbs drop in rings into the dusk
Of this November afternoon, as the flat, empty
Voice of the preacher drops the enormous words
Into the pit of absence—

          I am the Resurrection
And the Life, that whosoever believeth in me
Shall never die

      —but cannot fill it up.

What immortality should follow the life
Of one who, even living, seemed immortal,
A small, neat man who remembered everything.

No, the old script no longer carries conviction—
Not to these gray-headed people who have hunted
For diligent lifetimes the imaginary monster
Truth. They sit in embarrassed silence, wanting
To see their friend again, while the formulae
Of empty honor drone over their bowed heads—
And blind hope clamors in the dark outside.

CLASSIC EARTH: RECORD OF AN ITALIAN JOURNEY

1. The Umbrella-Pine, Nervi, August '53

Fruit of the unfruitful
And indifferent sea, rising slantward from a heap of shells
On the barren slope,
You raise your flat and spiny top where only the wind tells
A rasping ancient tale.

You are not beautiful,
But spare and scaly and strong; not gracious but stiff with years—
An old man whose hope
Has hardened into courage, as into stone his tears.
I know you will not fail.

2. Gothic Saint, Battisteria, Pisa

Crouched, melancholy, almost
Obliterate stone, what do
You await here? Some few
Short centuries won, or lost
By those who pass, and then
The Resurrection? Left
Backed to a round wall, reft
Of motion, music, again
From broken chains to rise
And sing—the withered mouth
Flowering after long drought,
New light in the blind eyes?

3. Cypress

Green flame,
From dark earth fed,
Dark flame,
Twisting, tight and straight,
Break through, break forth—
What sullen wood contained,
Contained no longer;
Dance, dance like a dark-haired girl,
Feet flying in a fragrant wind;
Rise, and be new.

4. On the Gray Hill

On the gray hill above Florence, misty with olives,
I sit in the open car-door, my feet in the grass,
And hear from the deep, domed valley a mellow confusion
Of bronze and silver, calling the folk to Mass.

Here, where the golfers walk and the lovers tangle,
Their antique postures revealing a present need,
No-one's alone, none either separate or single;
Spirits surround us, to which we pay no heed.
On the burned sod over Buonarotti's towers,
The dead dance on; the living can lie still,
Balanced at ease between upper and nether powers,
Brought into one accord on this high gray hill.

5. Statue of Saint Cecilia in Her Tomb, Rome

Beneath the altar, like a sleeping beast
That hunters have intruded on, she lies,
Legs virginally shut, arms stretched out stiff
To ward off yielding, and the twist of her throat
Pressing her mouth to kiss the clammy granite.

Deny, deny, her silence cries; deny
The moonlight streaming in, the frescoed heaven
Above my bed, its naked cherubim
Ready to drop on me their impudent flesh.
Who has defiled my house? Deny, deny.
Poor girl, poor Christian, to have desired so much—
Music, and miracles, and martyrdom
In high patrician style—and to reap only
The worship of gaunt harried washerwomen
Shuffling in dirty boots across your floor
Of polished stone like glass. Do you laugh or weep
To see your marble corpse so desolate?

6. Roman Etching: Piazza Navona

Here I see only ancient river-majesties
Flowing in marble green with flowing water,
And gold-brown houses mellow with age and sunlight,
Good wine and wisdom.

No grinning sign affronts me; in this elliptic
Heaven of stone no bar nor loan-office
Disturbs the fine firm line, as graven in copper,
Work of the craftsman,

Dividing the earth from sky, Man from the Cosmos
Which rolls above him, clouds in symmetric patterns
Reflecting the lower in the upper order,
Praise to the builders!

7. Tarquinia: Carmen Etrusca

1

Here is a middle kingdom underground,
Upon whose walls these painted dancers tread,
    Letting no sound
        Disturb these dead,
Crumbled at air's touch, or their spirits fled
To islands beyond sea, the world around.

Death is these joyful things: the banquet spread,
The maiden willing, the sound of flute and lyre,
    The leaf-crowned head,
        The sacred fire
Rising like fumes of strong wine ever higher
In the bright blood, till, the last garment shed,

The dance breaks forth in solemn liberty,
Investing the old flesh with a new dress;
    The agony
        And weariness
Of spent limb lifts, and lo, the unbound tress
Floats on the winds of passion joyously.
If then in dying they partake such pleasures
As, living, time and use obstruct and dim,

What wonder they dance death to lascivious
    measures
And celebrate it with a sensual hymn?

2

These horses live in form, and, pacing here
Among the trees, formal in branch and leaf,
    They know no fear
        Nor pain nor grief.
They are complete; their lives, however brief,

Move with the rhythm of the turning year.
The youths who hold their bridles, slim-hipped,
     straight
As trees themselves, move their hieratic limbs
   To celebrate
      With gestured hymns
The solemn change by which the strong sun dims
His shining, then burns forth regenerate.

And all the wild wise beasts, swimming or flying
Or coursing in the figured forest there,
   The swallows crying
      On crystal air,
And the lone fox's bark, call us to share
The mystery in their living and their dying.

How glorious, chaste, and happy all the world
Is here revealed!   What vision of delight!
This standard, in the face of Death unfurled,
Moves in no wind, will drop into no night.

8. The Bound Slaves of Buonarotti, Vatican Museum

Non ha l'ottimo artista alcun concetto
ch'un marmo solo in se non circonscriva
col suo soverchio; e solo a quello arriva
la man che ubbidisce all'intelletto.
[Even the best sculptor has no concept which is not already contained within a particular block of marble, and all that the hand, obeying the intellect, can do is to reveal the hidden form.]

M. Buonarotti,   *Sonnetto XV*

1
Not yet emerged, O thrusting spirits, not yet free,
Treading the stone beneath your dancing feet,

Nor slipped the lingering leash, nor sprung the trap,
Vaulted the mind forth of its firmament,
Winged from its marble tomb—oh not yet knowing
The full and searing blast of liberty,
You strain against substance, the humped strength of your shoulders
Shifting the very earth. Blind eyes uplifted
Stare forward through the whirling years at us,
Prisoned beholders, passing in these hushed halls
Between two glories, sharing neither. Loose
For all our sakes the bonds which lock those limbs
In thoughtless stone. Although we cannot know it,
We are as you, awaiting mind, hand and chisel
To strip away our hard integument,
And listening for the tune will set us dancing.

2

What—shall the hand of God the craftsman fail
Before the sun's in place, or the fixed stars
Show forth the whirling night? Shall the hand fail
Which is my hand, the thought which is my thought,
This work, this world still incomplete, undone,
Struggling in stone's fixed chaos to be born?
No: rather break the mold, the elements
Scattering as at first in their crude atoms
Through matter's oceans.

                        The form lives in the mind,
Which rots with age and sickness and disappointment;
The substance only is invincible.

Now wait upon me the stiff, gnarled, halting years,
The grating voice, the clouded eyes, the limp,
The sinews slackened, and the ruin of hope;
And I must leave the brave old Pope half-buried,
Borne to his tomb by weeping cherubim,

Surrounded by a wreck of noble thought.
Creation's scattered; my prophets, saints, and gods—
The fragments of my vision and my body
—Here and there aimless like lost dogs they travel.
My Moses sits alone in the cold church,
Staring toward a blank wall, God's glory turned
Forever from him, and his tablets shattered;
And here in this barren hall the bound slaves strive
Toward the light which is not, and the reality
Which is unreal—the image of their death.

3

Master, strike shackles! After four hundred years
Let thy hand return from its dust to set us free,
Our dumb stone turn and sigh—awakening
From what sad dream?—our buried voices, singing,
Rise in the firmament like stars of morning
On the bright climbing tide. Loose thou our praises,
Like the twelve winds that dance about the sky,
Whooping and calling.
      No: the dead hand sleeps,
And the mind, though it lives and knows,
      it will not heed us.
Being no longer kin to flesh, as we are.

And you, beholders, mark where death has brought us,
And tossed us on this dry shore, naked, twisted
In contrapposto from your gaze. Light, light,
Light, know us not! Earth, bear our suffering weight
No longer! Sense, unlock the prison-house
Wherein you keep us pent! Death, break us back
To stone again, and let the bloody shards
Fall unremarked from your indifferent hands.

THE DYING MEDITATION OF
GIOVANNI PICO DELLA MIRANDOLA,
CALLED THE PHOENIX OF INTELLECTS

Our low life was the level's and the night's;
He's for the morning.
Robert Browning, "A Grammarian's Funeral"

Inscribed to Albert R. Vogeler, *amicus curiosae.*

The loneliness of this body of this death
Lies on me heavily, and toward the Other,
That Spirit of that Life which is to come,
I now must hasten.
               Approach, my good friends all;
Bring my books closer.
               Now to this bed, this room,
This center of the world, this troubled town
Seething with riot like an ill-governed soul,
I've come, as end of all my learned journeys,
Who've known all heights, all depths—the exaltation
Of the insatiate flesh, and of the mind
Spiralling upwards toward the farther light:
All this is gathered in so little space
That I can turn and touch the corners of it,
Who once flew with the angels.
               Well, better so
Than to live on, with Duke Lorenzo dead,
Angelo dead, and the good Barbaro dead—
My masters always, whose sweet society
Redeemed this sorry world, fit now for nothing
But trampling hooves of horses, and of soldiers

Who would not know one letter from another.
But halt, Sir Platonist; this is doubtful doctrine,
And I grow heated, which I must not do
For fear of dying in imperfect mind.

Bereshith, in the beginning, saith the Kabbalah
In many-layered speech, was the Word always:
Verbum creator, sprung from the mind of God,
Without which naught was made—a tenfold emanation
Of which we catch the latest, faintest whisper,
But still enough to turn a man to cinders.
Bereshith—in that one all-pregnant word
Lie nested, as the tree within the seed,
Pater, et Filius, et Spiritus Sanctus,
Death, and Salvation, and the bleeding Cross.
Time was, I thought I might be one of those
Elected spirits, whom these high mysteries
Call with their strong bronze bell to know and serve them;
But that's all vanity, saith the unbelieving
Preacher, and the faithless Pope told me the same.
The fear of the Word was on him; he would have silenced
Its roaring in the solemn courts of Rome.
Vain man, thought conquers you! If not mine, then others',
And if not now, there's time on this wandering earth
Before the sun grows cold, and the Word is stilled.
But what a pain was there.
                         I am not
That perfect and spherical beast which Plato dreamt of,
That lacks both mouth and arse, and is eternal.
Therefore, to business.
                      As for my poems—such trifles
As youth must scribble, and wiser years repent of—
Let them stand monument to the vanity

Of worldly fame. Time was, the ladies swooned
In the public streets as I passed singing them.
Who'll hear them now? Only from those Conclusions,
Which troubled the Pope so with their long hard words,
May I expect renown—not for the things done,
But for the thing attempted. Friends, I tell you
That all my wakeful labors will seem child's play
Some centuries hence, and all my studied speeches
Prattle of children playing at being gods.

Most various Man, how shall all time suffice
For all thy praise? Even above the angels,
Fast-fixed ever in static adoration,
Thy mutable nature exalts thee. How celebrate
Worthily this chameleon, Proteus,
Mountebank, masquer, never twice the same?
If this the creature, what then the Creator?
What mind can frame Him, what spirit reach His height,
Or span His breadth, or plumb His shining depth?
What can we say of Him but that He *is*?
Still, though there are no maps, I've travelled there,
Feeling my way like blind men. Long I disputed
Whether God *sit intelligens, vel intellectus,*
Concluded, with Dionysius, he was neither;
Yet I must understand, or burst my skull
With all the weight of paper crammed within.

Incomprehensible Lord, grant me to know
Thy nature if I can, and see Thy face—
Though swathed in smoke by day, in flames by night,
And indistinguishable in seas of brightness
—Before the Dark which is Thy servant takes me.
Ain sof, the Rabbis called Thee—without an end:

A chasm filled with light, in which the mind
Flounders and drowns, then, like the gasping swimmer,
Rises the third time, bearing brighter treasures
Than others safe on shore ever attain to.

The moving image of eternity,
Reflected on the round walls of our world,
Approaches the center, and its intersection
With its true model; my time is growing short.
So much undone!
          Somewhere a manuscript
Lies waiting for my hand—it will wait long now—
That holds the universal key, resolves
The blinding flash of uncreated light
That burst upon me all those years ago
Into a legible pattern:
          All is one!
Hebrew and Chaldee and Magus Zoroaster,
The mystic Greek, the careful Stagirite,
Paul, Origen, Augustine, Fathers in conclave,
Speak all one language, if I could but learn it.

The mind in reaching forth consumes itself
Like to the Arab bird they've named me for;
Well, in five thousand years I'll rise again
And go to studying, but now I'm tired.
You will excuse me, friends—just for a moment?
Malach adonai Sabaoth...
        Domine
*—Qualunque sia—in manibus tuis commendo
Spiritum meum*
        Ora pro nobis, Maria.

POEM FOR A MODERN WEDDING

1

Our good friends all, gathered here to wish us well
As we salt the bluebird's tail, how shall we thank you
For your faith in us, and in the headlong beast
On whose back we ride, toward goals we cannot see?
In this cynic time, when Love's a castaway
On the barren ocean of thought, his very being
And name denied, insulted, blown forth on the empty air
In long hard words which tell us nothing, but leave
A bitter stench in the nostrils, it's good to be
With friends assembled to let the time remind them
Who Love is, and what service is due him, and what
Power he holds still, though now declined in fortunes.

Let none say Eros is dead. No: maimed and sleeping,
He gathers his wingéd strength to assault once more
The bastions of sorrow set in the bones.
Like all great gods, he dreams our world to being
Anew each morning, the world which greets our waking,
Dappled with shifting shades and shapes and colors,
And sounding with unheard music to his plucked bowstring.

2

Once, happy ancients, who knew in their marble bones
How things should be—counters of syllables
And builders of cities, who set the winds to music—
On such an occasion as this would have raised a tune
To set Olympus and the wild beasts dancing.
But who are we, with one era dead beneath us,
And the next not yet begun, to try such heights of song?
Poised on this sinking shoal of time, with signs in the sky

To show us change of seasons and dynasties,
We must look backward to the lost high plateau
Of youth and joy, or forward into the shifting fog
Which is our only horizon. Where is the breadth
Of view our fathers had? Where are the bearded gods,
Each solitary in his blaze of light, seeing only
The certainty of his own continuance?
Friends, we are fallen away from that good life;
Our children alone can regain it. Therefore this rite,
By which we now appease the denying demon
Who sets spirit warring against her brother flesh,
Stifling the ungrown seed in the womb of oblivion.

3

To lovers, locked and rocked in the hollow vessel of night,
The stars show no courses, and the winds are still.
No sextant have they, transit, nor astrolabe:
Hands reaching and touching, flesh opposed to flesh
Only must guide their solemn pilgrimage
Across the Elysian quicksands, by many dangers
Racked, wrecked, and wrestled; by Scylla and Charybdis—
The tearing tide, and the dry shore of drowning.

Friend Eros, helmsman of deeps, strong, patient hunter,
Whom none escape but to their sorrow, help us
Who lie wound in toils of nightfall, groping with hands
Feeble with imperfections, trembling with guilt and fear,
Toward that last perfect secret you promised us.
First god of all, hope of all breathing life,
Creator, illuminator of our dark world,
Lord of all pain, and of that painful joy
Wherein the sad self dies, and is renewed:
Shelter us, hovering over; grant us your peace.

THE CON-GAME: CLASSICAL ODE ON THE UNREALITY OF ALL THINGS

Oh shining imperial city, shelter us, who believe
        your riddled ground is firm,
though fault-lines run crisscross beneath your towers,
        extinct volcanoes erupt
through your pavements, and fetid marsh-water
        laps the foot of your wall.
You, unreal city, deceive us everywhere—
        on winter streets that answer
bright buildings with a flicker of watery light;
        or in the park where lovers
lie stretched upon the brown grass of late summer,
        and the birds sing them false
in dowdy branches, singing the lie how youth
        never fails utterly, how
love burns as the body lasts, and is not consumed.

        Wherever we go,
our blank mistaken faces staring up to signs
        in the low heavens, deception
is our road and destination out of the fosse
        where we else wander. We
do not know how by our errors we are saved.

    The gangster and the lunatic
present themselves as princes, millionaires,
        heirs to tall thrones and fortunes
in the distance. They say things which are not,
        but only by infection
from the false ground they stand on—the quicksand under
        illusion's asphalt floor.
And who can hear the lie in the impostor's
        smooth voice, or in the crank's
pronouncement, the mistake? Who but the grieved, eternal
        spectator of dissolution?

FROM HOSPITAL

1. Night on the Ward

A hypodermic and a drink of water
And a prayer for coolness, are the signs of day's end
In this captive world. Not silence: the machines
That keep the life in us still whir and clack.
Not darkness, for the nurse's night-light burns
Above her desk, a single votive candle.

The friendly pain, like the bears of infancy,
Accompanies us back to the dark world
Where not even we ourselves have ever been,
Nor can tell by the moss on the trees which way is home.

Let each hold the bright thread by which life hangs,
Across the dark hours and into tomorrow morning,
When the washbowls clatter, announcing the Resurrection,
And the nurses' shoes squeak brightly on the floor.

2. Death and Bingo

At seven o'clock last night, the old man died.
While we were playing bingo, shouting the numbers
In mush-mouthed southern speech, his final throw
Was called; he choked and left us, but without sorrow.
He was a bitter old man, who fought and quarrelled
To his last breath; the enemies outside,
The pain within pursued him night and day—
The hole in his throat that would not let him live,
The cruel mercy that would not let him die.

Goodbye, old friend—although you hated us all;
Tell them up there how it was here, and maybe

They'll give you clean sheets twice a day, and nurses
Who'll know what you want though you can't say it, and doctors
Who'll let you have it, though it's not good for you.

3. Delirium

The old man lay in his crib-bed like a baby's
And talked to phantoms walking stealthily
Out of the dark and Indian woods of youth.
"Knock three times; then come forward." The command,
From some forgotten ceremony, uttered
At depth of night in his strong voice, startled us
Who lay between cold green walls, thinking of nothing.
How much life boiled within that fleshless head
Those withered limbs, that fluttered, fading heart!

When, later, they pulled the curtains round the bed,
Covered it with a sheet, and pushed it forth
Into the hallway, I thought how the old man now
Could join his lost companions in their circle
And call upon the initiate, like himself,
To knock three times, and enter out of darkness.

4. The Orderly

He carries oxygen in the dead of night—
A tired, complaining *deus ex machina*
Guarding the lives of others, despising his own.
If you wake, you'll hear him quarrelling with the nurses,
Cursing the management in respectful whispers,
As he lounges in blood-stained khakis against the desk.

The rent, the cardiac wife, the starving children
—He would quote Hobbes if he could—are all gone through,
A weary catechism. Yet which of us here

Would not change places with him, to walk this moment
Free from this clean tomb out to the humming town,
And stop, and listen, and look at a healthy face?

5. This Seeing the Sick: for Ruben

When they brought you up from surgery, the stink of ether
Swathing your head like the nimbus of bright brown hair
Spread over the pillow, I thought I had never seen
More pitiful or lovely thing. Your flushed
Face of a dreaming child, turned to one side,
Rejected the pain of your awakening,
The poison within your flesh, the indignity
Of lying there, one white leg stuck in space.
And I thought: Such a son would I wish; no other.

But when you woke, and retched the poison forth,
And moaned with loneliness, and cried for water,
I was already leaving; the outer world
Had claimed me, and the different life of those
Who pass by suffering with averted eyes.
I could not help you now, as you had helped me
Those days before, when I lay bound and retching,
Send messages into that heedless world:
Was I still loved, or was I unremembered,
As good as dead and buried?
               Oh, this was treason!
Before the cock crew, thrice had I denied thee.

6. In the Next Bed
(for J. L., I.P.M.R. 2/14/57)

At one in the morning, the Divine Idiot
Talks to me, leering through the hospital window
In the lights of the waking city. My waste limbs

Twitch with remembrance like a sleeping hound's.
Believe, believe, the Idiot's voice intones
In the sounding stillness; believe it wasn't my fault
What happened to you; believe some other hand
Threw down upon you the weight that broke your back;
Please don't blame me; I'm blamed for everything.
I call the nurse to banish the Idiot's face
—The empty eyes, the open, slobbering mouth—
With cold hands to bring back other days
When among fellows I swung on easy shoulders
The load that since has crushed me to the earth,
Or feasted on flesh of women, drank draughts of sunlight,
Begetting brightness in the blood.
                      Oh God,
Whom I cannot believe, or must go mad,
Send me the nurse Death, with her cool touch dissolving
Caked fury from my bones, leading me home
To the dark cool cavern back at my beginning.

7. Visiting-Hours

Ambassadors arrive, bearing credentials
In paper bags, from the world outside these walls—
The springtime streets aswarm with singing lovers,
The lamp-lit houses waiting for tomorrow.
And some here have forgotten these, and listen
Absently to the eager relatives,
As if to the sound of distant battle-drums.
But some hold fast to the memory, as fingers
Clutch at the soaking sheet, and the lost voice
Strives to reply out of its twisted depth.
Bend closer to catch the message.
                              But how can they tell
The secrets of their prison-house? They have forgotten

What language they once knew to tell them in.

The hour is past; the visitors leave their parcels
And, shedding this suffering with a shake of their shoulders,
Pass forth to the elevator, and so down
And out once more into the joyful air.

8. Escape

The trees again! The birds again! The sun,
High over Central Park glints on the tops
Of cars which pass like splendid noisy beetles.
I have come forth—with one arm still in plaster
And one thought still for unforgotten comrades
Left in the dark Republic whose neighbor-state is Death—
To be henceforth one with those visitors
Who came with unwilling tribute to our bedsides,
And yet not altogether, for I have passed
Through lands and seas uncharted by them: terrors
Of solitary childhood and—before my time—
Forsaken, dumb old age.
         If I forget you
Now, my co-mates and brothers in exile,
I am not worthy of my own escape.

PROCESSION AT PEREDELKINO:
THE FUNERAL OF BORIS PASTERNAK, FROM A PHOTOGRAPH

As in a classical painting, the extended vista,
With the feathered trees in the foreground, boxes the eye
By leading it outward, and dwarfs the solemn file
Bound for the churchyard. The priests with their bells, the pallbearers—
The country neighbors, who knew only the man
Fond of his garden, and of brisk walks on bright mornings;
The city friends, in their dark suits ill at ease
Among summer fields, hearing still the great voice chanting
Out of the earlier years—all are swallowed in landscape.

The mourners are bringing home the internal exile
To the Russian earth, which, like the sea, remains,
Whatever winds pass over it, or waves frothing
Fly from its surface. His body will be lost there,
In distance lost and illimitable of clouds and grass;
And the wind's great riddling voice will blend with his
Over the whir of machines, and the dry command
From the brass throat of God.
        When a poet dies,
What is it they bury? Only the flesh that was suffered,
From habit, like a bad servant, long after the flame
Died in it with an empty whisper?
        Swinging their censers,
The slow priests chant for the soul's peace, and the mourners
Remember love, and the snowy spaces of youth,
And listen,   behind the rustle of their footfalls,
For the wind in the crackling thorns of history.

THE ROAD TO THE MOUNTAIN
(Pueblo to Aspen, 8/6-7/60)

1. Pueblo to Canon City

Leaving the town, passing the vacant lots
Of timothy and goldenrod, and tracks
Where wires follow, catching themselves up,
The bright dust follows us, wheeling and whirling
To the edge of the flat brown world, cinched in with mountains.

Spear-straight, bone-bare our road, and lonesome as
Thin voices singing in the smoky distance:
Oh give me a home.

      Here, mesquite and stunted poplar,
And sharp gray flints like fallen thunder tumbled
Into the dry arroyo, breaking its course;
Here, the road slices across the shattered country
Like truth or an open wound;

                up there, it jackknifes
Like a killed snake, and plunges into the hillside
With a shower of stones and a trickle of water.
                             Wait:
A road is its destination; where we are
Is where we are going—straight up the side of the mountain.

This, in a season of drought, is coyote's country,
Fixed in the moon; is not man's world, nor time's,
Nor ours, nor the machine's that makes a road,
At our impatient bidding, scratching and biting
The scaly earth.

      Only the rat and the lizard,
And the other small beasts of prey, yelping and scuttling
Belong in this place, for they draw the water of life

Out of their own thirsting flesh. The rest of us—
Great lumbering mechanisms of bone and gristle
—Must pull it with ropes out of the stubborn ground,
And carry it, cunningly caught in glass and metal,
Or else we dry in the wind to a feather's weight,
And blow away, like shades of other bones.

2. Canon City to Salida

Up through the wind-bitten canyon the river follows,
Gray-green as alabaster, white-flecked with stones,
Crisscrossed with flotsam branches, and choked with gravel.
And our road follows, one edge banked on the talus
The other rooted in cliffside, where willow and juniper
Project like crippled begging hands to block
Our upward course. Small water, all but lost
In sun-glare among tangled rocks, must guide us
In this precarious passage, out of the plain
Into the blind and shining sky. We rise,
Slowly, with hesitations, on swells of heat
Toward a new region where the cloudbank lowers
Veils on the sun, and rivulets spill on the roadway.

Unknown to us this world; in our former lives
The sun was with us always, and the mirages
Followed each other like cards flipped from a deck:
Here is the dark prince, here the danger from water,
And there is El Dorado, blinking with neon.
But this is real; this water can freeze the bone,
This resin-smell sting the nostrils, these rocks draw blood
As points strike flesh.
        Climbing, we leave behind us
Puffs of dark smoke—the bitter emanations
Of our transcended selves—and spurts of gravel
Clattering downslope toward streambed, stirring the echoes.

This is the place of change: the canyon opens,
Walls peeling away on each side like flower-petals;
Our river wanders off; our road strikes out
Over a new plain, but bending and weaving now
Between hummock and mesa—a faint, farther reflection
Of the lost stream's winding pathway. The desert is gone—
Left smoking below, with its thousand adaptive monsters.
Brown water runs in the ditches; storm-clouds gather,
And over there, the windows of a town
Reflect the brightness like an idol's eyes.

3. Buena Vista to Aspen—Independence Pass

From the tawny town, looking up, the road we will travel
Is scratched on the mountainside with a weaver's shuttle.
How we will rise to that height, the eye cannot tell,
Nor, by what turns and changes then descending,
From where we will emerge. The labyrinth
Invites, repels with cryptic signs and gestures,
As if a man danced on a parapet,
Beckoning others to jump. High heat-haze shimmers
Way up above there, where vision melts into light,
Peaks into burning sky, life into death.

Now the last climb; now, with a jolt, the pavement
Slides out from under us; the snake's last wriggle
Jars loose the last of the thoughts we have brought with us
From the lower world. The forest closes in—
Spruce, willow, maple, birches, quivering aspen
—Over our heads, at the first leap of the road,
Where pebbles skid and skitter, and brown dust rises
Against the following sun. Frail shadows of trees,
Upright as noontide, flit spiderly over the windshield,
Stirred by the resinous breeze of our wake, washed out
By passing unseen clouds.

                    Fat cattle, in the clearing,
Lean up the slope, to watch with indifferent eyes
The labor of our going: they were before
Us in these pastures, and can afford to wait
For rain, or for a change in the road's course,
Or for the end of the world, whichever comes first.

Now, suddenly, the blind eye sees.
                    True light,
Though flawed with shifting treetops, soaring birds, high clouds
And other actual things, floods down upon us.
But that is from up there;
                    here there are only
Bare rock and withered grasses, patches of snow,
And a sign saying that we can go no higher—
Not on these engines.
                    As stones poised to be thrown
Into the void, to measure its depth by the echo,
We stand for a moment, staring into the wind
That shuts our eyes with cold tears;
                    then down, down, down,
Into the valley which is the home of man
Where music sounds, and the beasts that know our language,
But scorn to speak it until we learn theirs,
Welcome the pilgrims home.

THE CAT OF BASTET

(Egyptian, Ptolemaic Period)

Abstract and wise, this three-planed head: the eyes,
Laughing, let pass no shadow of the death
Crouching inside. This pinch of dust subsumes
The soft voice of the beast, its cushioned claw,
The neck's firm arch, the forward-jutted ears.

Upright in this bronze coffin the embalmer
Closed the pure, holy lust, the cruelty,
Innocent as the wind, and blind as fate,
All strength, grace, beauty of the unhuman world,
Which lived, laughed, leaped the centuries through—until
They funneled themselves forever to this shape—
By that dim altar where the cat-priestess tore
Her lovers limb from limb.
      Sweet, swift beast, pacing
So silently those basalt-columned halls,
Not even the restless muttering dead awaken:
Do you like it there, chasing the dust of mice,
Lapping the milk dried in the bowl of years?
Or do you miss the moonlight, the smell of blood,
The tearing noise of passion in the throat?

DEO GRATIA: THE RECLUSE

I have forgotten the wind, the world, the way
Beyond the crossed bars of my cage, the reasons
Why I am here, the wash and sway of seasons
Over the blind stone.   I have forgotten day,
Where it divides from night, and the healed scar
Sunlight makes on the earth.   Here there is only
The light proceeding from the farthest star
At the back of my skull.

       Elect and proud and lonely,
I wait with folded hands for the novice's tread
On the sweating flags, the whisper of absolution
Behind the locked grate. Still breathing, I am dead,
And can achieve no further resolution
Of my mankind. What can the deaf priest say
To absolve me from the sins that are not mine?
I would forget the taste of heavenly wine,
And remember again the wind, the world, the way.

CHINESE PAINTING:
TRAVELLERS IN A MOUNTAIN PASS

(T'ang Dynasty; attributed to Li Ch'ao K'ao, called "The Little General")

These tiny, round-rumped horses, bucking beneath
Impossible crags, the little general painted,
Working a day as he lay in the piebald sun
Under the *t'ung* tree in the Emperor's garden.
Working a night in fog over Yangtze's reaches,
And, on the dry parade-ground, imagining waterfalls
From such far heights that the mind shatters, like water
Thrown from a black rock's blade in glistening fragments.

Men, animals, colors dance on the mellow silk
In time to the quiet breathing of the spirit
Behind the landscape, and the little general's brush
Keeps time with all of these. Oh, the minuscule joy
Of those pack-asses rolling in grass, their burdens lifted;
And the tiny splendor of the Emperor, riding
On his white palfrey up that defile of rocks!
All praise to the picture-maker, honor to his hand
That brought this life to birth, but glory to the spirit—
Slow, silent, smiling, immortal—in whose name he worked!

BACK YARD, BERKELEY, LATE MARCH

1

The fence-boards shudder in the harsh spring light.
Eyes dazzle with lost gulls against the clouds,
Like flecks of blood caught in the living crystal.

2

The wind that tosses the gulls I cannot feel
—It is too high, too far; it is not mine—
Nor the force that clothes with white the thorn-tree bough
In the neighbor's yard, nor what it is that shakes
The dry wood of the fence beneath my hands,
Although there is no wind here.

3

But I can feel the strength that hides the sun, quenches the light,
Stops still the turning blood, the flying clouds,
Within the waiting eye shatters the crystal.

4

The gulls, if I could hear them, would cry: Change, change!
Too late! The wind is gone, and so are we.
The thorn-tree has cast its blossoms and stands bare;
The earth no longer shakes; the fence is still
Under the clutching hands of an old man.

CHICAGO HASH-HOUSE NOCTURNE, MID-NOVEMBER

'Bye now; hurry back.
                 — and out into the rain
Under the elevated,   slanting down
Through weeping clouds of light.
                 I had not known
Life had undone so many.
                 The blank gale off the lake
Has wiped the sidewalks clear,   polished our faces
Of all humanity,   now hurtles onward
With nothing more to do. Inside, the diners
Hunch over their carrion,   munching silence,
Withstanding the clatter,   the curses,   the ticking,   exploding
Hearts under crumpled suits.
                 But is this all?
And how were we to have known that it was all
When we entered screaming out of the pouring street?

THE GREENLAND FISHERMEN

Northward into the sun of darkness, into the formless cold,
Where the fog surrounds us like the fields of home,
We have sailed, singing of oxen and olive-groves,
Remembering wine on the lips, and barefoot girls,
And the sun, warm on the lizard-sheltering stones.

In the dark beneath us, the snub-nosed cod pass by
Through a forest of hooks, their steely heads ringing faintly
With the cold smell of home.
                      Our lines measure our life:
As we follow them down, we come again to childhood—
The feel of a clean bed, and the laughter of friends.

But where is our home?
                      The silent compass wanders
Like a crazed woman by the sea-strand, crying
The words of a prayer against the on-shore wind.
What will our shelter be—the ice-blocked port,
The killing storm, the gray-green shore of death?

We drift, unknowing as are the fish we prey on,
In the wake of the ice-floe, north-northeast with the current;
The sun goes out like a blown candle; the ship's bell
Clanks dully against the fog-wall, calling us back
To humankind from the indifferent sea.

THE HUMMINGBIRD: A LESSON IN OPTICS

The hummingbird inches along his invisible string
   Through sunlit space, dashing from shade to shade,
     Pausing at death, then moving on. The air
Invisible with morning shines through his wing,
   And shone already before our world was made,
     And we could see it. To him, we are nowhere,
Though we can see him, and we know we are here,
  Though he cannot see us.
                He stitches the world
   Together—hitch! stitch! rich!—against the attack
Of the hidden sun. Although the sky is clear
  Its light is known to us only as fragments hurled
     To the dry ground like spear-shards.
                The hummingbird's track
Bisects the sun-rays.
                Look! Is what we see
  What's really there? And what then of the bird's
                Blank garnet eye? Does it take in a light
  Which ours cannot—which we must catch with words
For want of wings?
                The hummingbird's string floats free
  In the dappled air.
                Whither the mind's true flight?

DREAM VISION: A DOOR OPENS

As if a visitor
were due to arrive by foot from a far journey,
at a time uncertain, but his arrival certain,
and we stood waiting,
behind the front window, for the jut of his head
above the horizon, the rustle of his footfalls
in the dry grass at the far end of the path,
the squeal of the screen door, and the sound of his voice
reporting to us from a distant country,
which we already know, where the crows fly backward,
prophesying the past;
                —so the future comes
walking toward us, itself unchanged, like a traveller, bringing
his thoughts from home, while we wait, unmoved, unchanging
from childhood into age;
                or as if we moved,
each silently and alone on a moving sidewalk,
through an immense space—gallery? railway-station?
—seeing always new parts of the same space,
new platforms with trains arriving with no-one on them,
new falls of light from the glass roof;
                so, whatever will be
is there already, but we have not yet come
to the place where it is, and whatever has been is still there,
but we have passed beyond it;
                till finally
we emerge from under the glass roof, into sunlight,
the moving sidewalk stops, footfalls echo on stone,
real trains arrive, bringing people, and the guest, bringing news,
closes the screen door behind him.

APPEARANCES OF THINGS:
FROM THE PATIO, SUNNY AFTERNOON
IN LATE MARCH

In the window, as I look in, I see reflected
The hummingbird-feeder, like a false jewel, hanging
Among the furniture of the dark room, bearing
The sunlight within itself. The trees behind it
—Dark against bright sky—print themselves on the glass
In negative.
       The sun, distant beyond them,
Hangs like a true jewel in the glass of darkness,
Starring its surface with remembered light.

And of all these, only eye and glass are real.

THE PROBLEM OF THE Nth JUMPER

No-one saw anyone jump; it was too dark.
No one found anything; there was too much water,
But a sea-bag containing id. was left on the deck
And a letter in mimeograph went to the papers:
>The world as it is, that is here, I cannot accept
>And the better world is not here. I do not know
>Whether it will be found in the dark water
>Rushing beneath my feet, or in the air
>Between where I am now and the wave, or in neither place,
>But I know that that world exists in my head, as this one
>Does not, and never has, and therefore I know
>Where I am going, although not where I am.

At first light the Coast Guard dragged the channel; the reporter
By telephone interviewed the pregnant wife
And the grieved, indifferent parents; the typesetter
Spread out the jumper's story among the ads
For cars, and cigarettes, and retirement homes
And over-the-counter drugs.
>Now, later, the commuters

And cabbies and shopping housewives glance at the story
With splintered vision, as they go, like mourners,
About the streets, for they know, unlike the jumper,
Where they are now, but not where they are going,
But, like the jumper, they know the better world
Is still out there somewhere, though no-one yet has found it.

THE CITY OF EARLY FALL:
OLD MAN IN THE PARK

Sun, before failing, warm my mortal bones
Against the wind out of the opposite corner.
As I sit here—friends gone to their long homes
Out of the wind's way, closer, safer, warmer

Than I ever was—it cuts through my thin coat
As the sun throught he cold slats scratches my shoulderblades.
Pressed between light and darkness, looking out
On an emptying earths let me say: nothing abides.

Not even you, sun; not even the I which is eye,
And does the looking; nor the lovers curled
On the brown sod like fallen leaves.
                So high
You stand above me, sun, you know my world

Only as I might know the world of the fly
Which crawls my withered hand. Yet sun and man
Must fail at the one moment: you in the sky,
Stooping behind a cloud; I as I stand
Among these blown leaves and this drifting dust,
Honed by the wind till only my gaze remains
Like a smooth hard stone. I live because I must
And while I must, before my thin blood drains
Down through cracked asphalts and my shallow breath
Beats weakly against the wind, repeating: Death.

SUMMER EVENING IN THE SUBURBS:
WAITING FOR A MOVIE

Here, gathered on the pavement in front of the dream-house,
The kids in their bright tank-tops, touching each other,
The bikers, freshly dismounted swinging their helmets,
The escaped housewives, slumped against the building
Murmuring like birds on their way to sleep.
—And we, in our wheelchairs, speaking to no-one, touching
No-one, are all united in expectation,
Not knowing what to expect.
        But if an angel
Were to arrive on the shopping mall, saying: Hosannah!
Know that the world you know no longer exists;
The new one is coming to birth in time for the nine-o'clock.
—All of us would turn slowly, with:—Hey, far out!
Or:—Why, look at that! Or:—I always knew it would happen
In just this way.
        —And then move smoothly forward
Into the new world beyond the pavement, just as we now
Move through the doors of the dream-house,
each one to his or her private
And insignificant revelation.

NOCTURNES

1. Questions With No Answers
(variation on a phrase by Robert Bly)

The question is not whether the song will continue
after the words have ended,   but what it will say
to those who stand in the clearing.   Not:
will the music sound?
but: Who will be there to hear it,
and, hearing, understand, and, understanding,
remember and reply? Will the voice be lost
between the dark trees and the darkening sky,
where the birds walk balanced on the last light, and
the stars await their turn?   The question is not even
so much what the song will say as how the silence
that follows it will be broken—by the wind of night,
the bird's last call, the last beat of the sun's
wings, or, to all these, the listening heart's reply.

2. After Catullus

While the horizon holds
and after the light departs, but while
we still remember it, I will proclaim
that the world's death shall be rescinded, but
not to our present vision, for tomorrow
we shall not be as we are now.
                    The eye
is not satisfied with seeing, nor the ear filled
with hearing, nor do the limbs
tire of feeling the world's breath upon them;
yet there is no
more time.

3. After Plato, from the "Greek Anthology"

The morning star, light of the living, becomes, when it dies,
   the evening star, and lights the world of the dead.

4. Through the Restaurant Window

The snake-path of the light on the dark water—
   the road of light into the mind.

LITANY OF THE TWO WORLDS

1

The dead are divided from us
by the glass wall of sense, so
that when they speak, we cannot
hear them—or only a word

here and there, swallowed, destroyed
by the roaring funnel of air,
the rattle of earth, the hiss
of falling stars. The dead are

divided from us by the slip
of time, the pale flash of two
glass panes sliding past each other—
shallow, sea-green when you look

through them the long way—so that
we cannot interpret their
gestures, or tell whether they
want to attract our attention
or are merely waving away
unwanted birds or insects
or worshipping gods unknown
on our side of the glass.

2

The dead are divided from us
by the colors of their sun,
which is dark in the middle
and bright around the edges,

as though in eclipse, and which
travels by night, and hides during
the day like a man crossing
a desert. The dead are divided

from us by the shape of their world,
where mountains fall into valleys
and the seas hang overhead—
whorled, green-veined with white, opaque

and ringing as malachite bells.
Yet, though the dead are divided
from us by these things, we infer
that they wish they were not, for when

one of us goes to join them
through the gate in the glass wall,
while we grieve, they rejoice, and will not
let the visitor return.

3

The dead are divided from us
not by our will or theirs, but
by the stairs of knowledge, leading
up and down in the walls of time

and back and forth in the glass wall
of sense, with shut gates. The dead are
divided from us as we are
divided from each other.

THE SHADOW AND THE LIGHT

1

For the shadow and the light are both equally real
    even when only one of them is seen,
as the sun, when it goes behind a cloud, still shines,
    although in secret; as the leaves in winter
still shine green in the dark tree-bark, though in potential
    only; as stars that died long since still shine
for us, who have never died until this moment; so
    the light inhabits the shadow, stretching its fingers
out to the edges of it, curling and curling within
    the black ball, as the snake within the egg.

2

    And both the light and the shadow are equally
unreal, even when both inhabit vision. Look
    where the sun splits the cloud bank, and its rays
descend like ladders along the cliff of air. Where is
    their substance? Who can climb such ladders—up
or down, hand over hand, wing under wing, bright earth
    to darker sky, to earth again—or stand
balanced on that gray rock hung above treetops?

3

We know how the shadow inhabits the bowl of light,
    as fish do an ocean, or as stars the sky
by daylight or on cloudy nights, waiting for us
    to see them, waiting to be, waiting for time
to bring them out of greater light—not greater, perhaps
    but at least closer and more visible—
or out of what seems to us darkness, as we stand blind here
    though it is full of light. But what the shadow
contains, what lies beyond it, what will become of it,
    we cannot know, for we dwell within the shadow.

SEEING ANGELS
(Story told by a Friend)

       It's no trick to see angels: I did it all the time
when I was a child. Sitting in church, one Sunday
after another, I'd watch them floating down
out of the choir-loft,
refracting white light through the tissues of their wings,
until the brown air blazed with colors, though there was no
stained glass.
       It was our neighbor's crazy daughter,
who had survived a massacre in the old
country, gave me the idea. She swore the angels had saved her,
plucking her like a flower out of the bare
and bloody ground; and afterwards she spoke
to crowds of shawled old ladies and wheezing old men
who never had seen angels, but wished they had,
or had seen them, but then forgotten.
As she looked down
into that sea of faces, she saw the angels
again, and was vindicated, and never returned
from that landing halfway to heaven, to join the rest of us.

       As I grew older, I no longer saw angels,
though I still knew they were there, for I had seen
them once.
       But, you see, the point is not
in seeing the angels only, but in knowing
what they mean, what they want of us, how to interpret
the rustle of feathers, the distant trumpet-call

—and of these things, old as I am, I know no more now
than did the children who first saw the angels.

THE FAILED PROPHET

Some time during the Last Days, God stopped speaking to me.
The heavens, which had been filled with sound, fell silent;
which had been filled with light, were darkened;
which had been filled with meaning, now went blank
as the mind of a stone.

What had been filled with power was now like a child's arm
thrown up to ward off a falling tree-trunk.

I walked out each morning expecting to hear, as before,
the clear command, although I could not do
the thing commanded, but now, though I could have done
whatever was wanted, it seemed that nothing was wanted.

The Last Days continued, but nobody seemed to notice;
the end came, with a soft lurch, as though a car
had reached the end of the pavement, but everything looked
just as it always had, except that when
I raised my hand before my face, I could not see it.

IMMIGRATION FILE

"Refugee Has Rare Chance to Be in 'Heaven'"
 The New York Times, 8/22/93, Sec. 1, p. 1

"And I alone am escaped out of all to tell thee."
 Book of Job

1. Report of the Unknown Refugee

I clambered up from the hold and blinked in the sunlight
of the new country.
 The helicopter was there
to take me ashore, leaving behind my comrades,
who had been in the hold with me, breathing the same foul air,
eating the same one meal every two days, wanting the same light.

A blue-eyed man stood in the helicopter's doorway,
gesturing toward me and saying: "Bring in that man,
and send all those others back to where they came from!"
And that was done.
 So now I sit in the anteroom
of the blue-eyed man's office, wearing a clean shirt
and somebody else's trousers, and wondering what I should say
to those who question me now, or when my children ask me,
in future years, how I got here.
 I cannot speak
the blue-eyed man's language, nor can he speak mine.
His thoughts are as strange to me as the Mandates of Heaven
were to my ancestors, and yet his mercy has pulled me
out of that stinking hold, into the sunlight,
into the clamor of history, into the circle
of his Elect.

2. Queries of the Rejected

We do not understand why only our comrade was chosen
to walk in freedom, and to see the new light

over these strange, rounded mountains, while we were sent back
along the watery pathways. Our eyes are shaped like his,
and see the same world. He stank as we do, after
those months of darkness and no fresh water.
        Where
is it written that only the blue-eyed shall say
who stays and who returns? What we desire
is only the same light our comrade has, for it
is written: "Around the Four Seas, all men are brothers."

        3. Testimony of the Blue-Eyed Man

My ancestors arrived in a sailing ship
in the gray dawn of another century
quite unlike this one.
        They travelled west with the new
land, in waves toward the western ocean, carrying roads
and railways rolled up in their pockets, and pushing tall buildings
ahead of them like hunters' blinds. It never occurred
to them, or to me either, that the land wasn't theirs
to do with just as they wished, or that those who came to it later
weren't there to help them do it.

When I got out of law school, there was a glut
of young men like me—in nice suits, with hair combed back,
wearing horn-rimmed glasses. I took what seemed the safest
job that was offered.
        I sat behind my desk until
my mind and my arms took root in it as it floated upward
out of the murky depths, into a place
of some sunlight, carrying me with it.
Now at last I stand in the helicopter's doorway,
on the freighter's shuddering deck, pointing and giving orders.
The people on deck see me, but not those who sent me,
and do not understand that although I give orders,

I must also take them; that although I apportion the light
to others, I don't control how much I get,
and that though I run the system, others decide
what it is, and what it does.

> 4. Statement of the Prisoner Awaiting Disposition

I am the one neither returned nor accepted,
but forgotten here, like wood piled up for the winter
by people who have moved away. From my cell, even rising on tiptoe,
I can see only a single street, and one pale
slice of the sky. My meals are sent to me
by unseen hands, through a hole in the metal door.
I collect my wastes in a pail, which I push each evening
out through the same hole, and get a clean pail in return.

I see no one, hear nothing.
> And now you come, with your notepad
and questions—no doubt, a different kind of official:
younger, perhaps, and less proud, but still with the pen and the glasses,
still with the same dark suit.
> And, like other officials,
you do not answer my questions:
> Is this the new country?
What did my ancestors see, who went to the Golden Mountains,
and returned as old men, with strange clothes and stranger stories,
to find their village shrunk to the size of a fishpond?
Is this why I crawled over the heaving water
as my comrade drowned beside me, and stumbled retching
up the rocky beach? Was all that for these bare white walls,
this metal door with a hole, this pail, and this clanging silence?

This much I could find at home.
> Something must be wrong.

PRELUDES

1. Dreams of the Maimed

It comes to me that the blind who once saw believe
That they will see again, because the world
They once saw is still out there, and that those
Whose ears have closed dream that they hear the ocean,
And, waking, hear it still, because the dream
Locked in their skulls continues. It comes to me
That those who once walked, ran, danced across the earth,
But now no longer, dream that they still have feet,
That curled toes grapple dirt, that wet grass rises
Above the ankle. It is in me that I
Dream none of these things, know and remember nothing
Save what my waking senses tell me, foresee nothing
Save more of what I know and am already.

It comes to me that the dead dream that they live.

2. Moment of Silence, Please

The voice of someone who has grown up with silence, hearing
   only the lizard's foot on the dry stone wall,
the cry of the unmated bird in the espaliered tree, which sounds
   in season and out, the grass in yesterday's wind,
the rustle of water in the dry stream-bed, and the faint
   electric hiss of sunlight on pale gray rock
this is the only voice that can confirm what I
   say here: that the sounds we hear all the time, the strumming,
 twangling music that fills the space in front of us,
   parting as we move through it, uniting behind us,
are only as the motes that swim in the air at first light,
   but, as the day advances, are seen no longer.

Blessed are they who hear what others do not, for they
   already know what others never learn.

THE WELL-BEHAVED OLD MAN'S
HALF-LAMENT FOR HIS OLD AGE

My hungry companion who was always with me,
following close behind, hissing and pointing,
saying: "Look there! See that? Let's see, can we get
some of what's over there?" has fallen way back.
Sometimes I barely hear his steps.

As I was eating dinner, or reading a book,
or talking with casual friends, saying: "Yes, that's the way
it's always seemed to me," the importunate fellow,
with a prick as long as his ears, would sit perched on my shoulder,
suggesting unspeakable things, which I never did.

Now, disappointed, he has abandoned me.
When I looked backward, I glimpsed him on the brow
of a hill, loping away into the distance—
and I was sad.
        Not that I ever liked him,
exactly—for I could never deliver his goods,
and that made me feel bad—but, somehow, with him gone,
I'm not the same, like a man with a missing arm.
In the country from which I came, the girls wore loose clothing
which swirled around them like mists—in patches of sunlight,
they lay with legs spread in the damp grass, waiting
for what would come—and the boys were lean and lively,
with red-gold glints in their hair, as they stepped lightly
among the scattered girls, greeting each with a smile and a kiss,
and promising more at sundown.
        But if that country ever
existed, it now no longer exists. Only my hungry
companion remembers it, from having walked there, and he

has taken his memories with him.
>   Is it time for me now
to sit with the other old men in the watery sunshine
of the old kitchen-garden, and complain that the world has grown weary
of warming us, that our chairs are hard, that the young men no longer
respect us, and that someone should come and call us to dinner?

FOURFOLD PRAYER

      Be with me, sun,
as my eyes close—a warm bright hand on my body,
shining and reaching through skin and thin blood, down
to where the shivering beast sits in the shadow
of the bone's arch.

      Be with me, wind,
pushing your fingers through the cloth at my shoulder,
prodding the beast awake.

      Be with me, sound,
of the earth turning—rustle of the heavens,
squeal of the sun in its blue box spattered with leaves,
the whirring of the blood behind my ear
spinning away to nothing.

      World, be with me.

VOICES FROM A WAR ZONE

1. Best of luck
   says the bemedalled general,
   to the novice pilot,
   preparing
   for his first sortie,
   drop your bombs in good faith
   as we always do,
   and let's hope to god
   they don't hurt anyone
   who isn't supposed to be hurt.

2. It seems, says the refugee
   on the road below,
   that I was born in the wrong place,
   and will presently die
   in a quite different place
   which is still the wrong one.

3. Those were some scary moments
   but on the whole
   not nearly as bad
   as I expected
   says the novice pilot returning
   from his first sortie.
   And just think of the returns—
   two laser-guided bombs,
   two puffs of black smoke
   from three miles below,
   and in return,
   four years of college, law school or med school,
   life-time health care,
   and a guaranteed home loan.
   Hell, that's a good bargain.

ABOUT THE AUTHOR

Stephen Porter Dunn was born March 24, 1928 to the geneticist L.C. Dunn and Louise P. Dunn. He struggled all his life with severe cerebral palsy. He was educated at Lincoln School of Columbia University; and as a boy and young man his parents provided him with the opportunity to travel in Norway, Sweden, France, England, Ireland, and Italy. He graduated from Columbia College with a B.A. in 1950 and received his Ph.D in Anthropology from Columbia in 1959 after conducting fieldwork among the Jews of Rome. On October 6, 1956 he married Ethel Deikman, a graduate of the Russian Institute at Columbia, who was also a victim of cerebral palsy. They called the event the Great October Revolution. (It was very unusual for disabled people to be married, and even more unusual for them to marry each other.)

For twenty-five years Stephen Dunn was editor of both *Soviet Anthropology and Archaeology* and *Soviet Sociology*, translation journals published by M. E. Sharpe, Inc. He translated two books by A. P. Okladnikov: *The Soviet Far East in Antiquity* (1965) and *Yakutia Before its Incorporation into the Russian State* (1970). He also translated three books by Alexander Yanov: *The Russian New Right* (1978), *The Origins of Autocracy* (1981), and *The Drama of the Soviet 1960s: A Lost Reform* (1984). He edited a number of translations, including *Peoples of Siberia* (1964), *Man and His Work* (1970), *Introduction to Soviet Ethnography* (2 vols., with Ethel Dunn, 1974), Ethel Dunn's translation of A. I. Klibanov, *The History of Religious Sectarianism in Russia (1860s-1917)* (1981), and he revised the English translation of *Popular Beliefs and Folklore Traditions in Siberia*, edited by V. Dioszegi (1968).

Stephen Dunn wrote four scholarly books: *Cultural Processes in the Baltic Area under Soviet Rule* (1966); *The Peasants of Central Russia* (with Ethel Dunn, 1967, reissued 1988); *Kulturwandel in sowjetischen Dorf* (with Ethel Dunn, 1977); and *The Fall and Rise of the Asiatic Mode of Production* (1982). He also wrote over one hundred articles and book reviews. Stephen and Ethel Dunn established Highgate Road Social Science Research Station, Inc., in Berkeley, California in 1969 as a non-profit foundation to support their scholarly work. He taught courses in the peoples of the USSR at the Monterey Institute of Foreign Studies, 1970-74, and the University of California, Berkeley; and at San Francisco State University in 1980 he taught comparative religion, his favorite subject. He published two literary works, *Prose and Verse* (with L.C. Dunn, 1950), and *Some Watercolors from Venice*, 1956. He died at his home in Kensington, California, on June 4, 1999.